Hotdish for the Heart

Casserole for the Soul

Jennifer Grant

ISBN: 978-1517316013

For my daughter, Jasny.

*Thank you for inspiring me
to continue reaching.*

I love you.

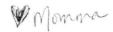

❧ Welcome ❧

At a life-changing seminar in 2009, I found myself holding a board that held my limiting belief of 32 years – "I'm not good enough." It was a symbol. I would be given the chance to break my board, thereby pushing through the limiting belief, propelling my life forward.

With my past, I was convinced my board would never break and yet, I also knew that IF it did break, my life would change dramatically. It took three tries, but when it finally broke, I quickly realized that the biggest reason was my mind. I also realized that the biggest thing that had held me back all those years was my mind. The thoughts I allowed myself to think were either going to hold me back and keep me stuck or they would allow me to move forward.

After that fateful day in Chicago when I broke my board, I knew I would need support in order to keep moving in this new direction. I began surrounding myself with an environment that was encouraging. My growth and transformation relied on new people, places and experiences. During this time, I also wrapped my mind with positive and inspiring words. Many of these words are featured on the pages that follow.

There are times in our lives when we need a little extra bump in the right direction. A push to keep us aligned and focused with where we desire to go. Sometimes, we need a full pick-me-up and a reminder of our worth. This little book is like a hotdish for YOUR heart; it warms you to the core and keeps you satisfied for hours. Filled with little bites of wisdom, each time you pick it up, you're opening yourself to a happier life.

It is my greatest intention that you always know the truth of who you are — light and love. You are uniquely designed and divinely created for something spectacular. The time is now for you to open up and embrace the gifts you've been given. Allow this little book to serve as a guidepost to support you on your journey forward.

Make a Difference . . . Lead with Love

The journey inward is the most
challenging you will ever face. It is also
the most rewarding.

- Jennifer Grant

The fact is there is nothing more
beautiful, more worthy, or more
conscious than you.

- Yogi Bhajan

If you are always trying to be normal,
you will never know how amazing you
can be.

- Maya Angelou

You have to know what sparks the light
in you so that you, in your own way, can
illuminate the world.

-Oprah Winfrey

I don't have to chase extraordinary moments to find happiness – it's right in front of me if I'm paying attention and practicing gratitude.

- Brené Brown

Yesterday I was clever, so I wanted to change the world. Today I am wise, so I am changing myself.

- Rumi

Unless you love and accept yourself
fully and completely, true long term
happiness will continue to elude you.

- Jennifer Grant

You must be the change you wish to see
in the world.

- Mahatma Gandhi

A loving heart is the beginning of all knowledge.

- Thomas Carlyle

People's lives are a direct reflection of
the expectations of their peer group.

- Tony Robbins

For cosmic career support, ask yourself whether what you do is a conduit for the good, the true or the beautiful. Don't look for your unique gift; look for your next loving thought.

- Marianne Williamson

One moment can change a day, one day
can change a life, and one life can change
the world.

-Buddha

Life is not a dress rehearsal.

- Rose Tremain

Be that which you are seeking and you'll no longer seek it. Desire love; be love. Desire happiness; be happiness.

- Jennifer Grant

I don't believe people are looking for
the meaning of life as much as they are
looking for the experience of being alive.

- Joseph Campbell

15

I am not what happened to me. I am
what I choose to become.

- Carl Jung

If you cannot fly, then run. If you cannot run, then walk. If you cannot walk, then crawl. Whatever you do, you have to keep moving forward.

- Martin Luther King Jr.

17

Your life doesn't belong to you but to everyone who will be touched by your light.

- Lisa Nichols

I have found the paradox, that if you love
until it hurts, there can be no more hurt,
only more love.

- Mother Teresa

In order to move through an obstacle we
must look beyond it. We have to look
past that which is holding us back.

- Jennifer Grant

And the day came when the risk to
remain tight in a bud was more painful
than the risk it took to blossom.

- Anaïs Nin

The golden opportunity you are seeking is in yourself. It is not in your environment; it is not in luck or chance, or the help of others; it is in yourself alone.

- *Orison Swett Marden*

Your life is the sum result of all the
choices you make, both consciously and
unconsciously. If you can control the
process of choosing, you can take control
of all aspects of your life. You can find
the freedom that comes from being in
charge of yourself.

- Robert Bennett

Travel light. Live light. Spread the light.
Be the light.

-Yogi Bhajan

24

People are always blaming their circumstances for what they are. I don't believe in circumstances. The people who get on in this world are the people who get up and look for the circumstances they want, and if they can't find them, make them.

- George Bernard Shaw

You can't make positive choices for the
rest of your life without an environment
that makes those choices easy, natural,
and enjoyable.

- Deepak Chopra

Keep in mind you never know the
impact you are having on the garden of
someone's mind. You may be planting the
seed, you may be nourishing the roots,
you may be watching as the life appears
above ground!

- Jennifer Grant

You can fail at what you don't want so
you might as well take a chance at doing
something that you love.

- Jim Carrey

The whole universal system is held together through love, harmony, and cooperation. If you use your thoughts according to these principles, you can transcend anything that gets in your way.

- Wayne Dyer

We teach best what we most need to
learn.

- Richard Bach

Have the courage to follow your heart
and intuition. They somehow know
what you truly want to become.

- *Steve Jobs*

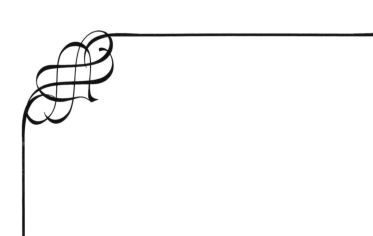

Where there is love there is life.

-Mahatma Gandhi

Life is not easy for any of us. But what
of that? We must have perseverance
and above all confidence in ourselves.
We must believe that we are gifted for
something and that this thing must be
attained.

- *Marie Curie*

33

Anybody can be great because anybody can serve. You don't have to have a college degree to serve. You don't have to make your subject and verb agree to serve. You only need a heart full of grace. A soul generated by love.

- Martin Luther King Jr.

34

Throughout your day you are constantly given moments to be grateful for, look and you will find them. Be open to the messages coming your way.

- Jennifer Grant

Joy is what happens to us when we allow
ourselves to recognize how good things
really are.

-Marianne Williamson

I was once asked why I don't participate
in anti-war demonstrations. I said that
I will never do that, but as soon as you
have a pro-peace rally, I'll be there.

- Mother Teresa

Holding onto anger is like grasping a hot coal with the intent on throwing it at someone else; you are the one who gets burned.

- Buddha

Strive for continuous improvement,
instead of perfection.

- Kim Collins

If you can imagine it, you can create it.
If you can dream it, you can become it.

- William Ward

Following a dream is like driving at
night. You see the road unfold only a few
feet at a time. You don't need to see the
entire road to know you are on the right
path.

- Jennifer Grant

I do not believe in miracles. I rely on them.

- Yogi Bhajan

Your vision will become clear only when
you look into your heart. Who looks
outside, dreams. Who looks inside,
awakens.

- Carl Jung

43

Intuition is a spiritual faculty and does
not explain, but simply points the way.

- Florence Scovel Shinn

We begin to find and become ourselves
when we notice how we are already
found, already truly, entirely, wildly,
messily, marvelously, who we were born
to be.

- Anne Lamott

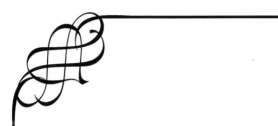

We're all just walking each other home.

- Ram Dass

I am only one, but I am one. I cannot do everything, but still I can do something. And because I cannot do everything, I will not refuse to do the something that I can do.

- Edward Everett Hale

Only when you're tired of being the
victim of your own life, can you the
wake up and be the hero of your own
life.

- Jennifer Grant

48

To forgive is to set a prisoner free and to discover that prisoner was you.

- Lewis Smedes

To love yourself right now, just as you are, is to give yourself heaven. Don't wait until you die, if you wait, you die now. If you love, you live now.

- Alan Cohen

Protect your spirit from contamination.
Limit your time with negative people.

- Thema Davis

Gratitude unlocks the fullness of life.
It turns what we have into enough, and
more. It turns denial into acceptance,
chaos to order, confusion to clarity.

- Melody Beattie

Your life is the fruit of your own doing.
You have no one to blame but yourself.

- Joseph Campbell

Abundance is a process of letting go; that
which is empty can receive.

-Bryant McGill

Being challenged in life is inevitable,
being defeated in life is optional.

- Roger Crawford

Having an impact does not require a title
or a label. Having an impact requires a
choice.

- Jennifer Grant

If we did all the things we are capable of,
we would literally astound ourselves.

- Thomas Edison

Courage does not always roar.
Sometimes courage is the quiet voice at
the end of the day saying, "I will try again
tomorrow."

- Mary Anne Radmacher

A failure is only a step on the way to
your success.

- Yogi Bhajan

The best way to find yourself is to lose
yourself in the service of others.

- Mahatma Gandhi

To plant a tree is an act of faith in the future.

- Michael Pollan

Some people come in your life as blessings. Some come in your life as lessons.

- Mother Teresa

If today were the last day of your life,
would you want to do what you are
about to do today?

- Steve Jobs

Faith is taking the first step even when
you don't see the whole staircase.

- Martin Luther King Jr.

In each and every moment we have the
option to see a new light, a new way.

- *Jennifer Grant*

Let yourself be drawn by the strange pull
of what you love, it will not lead you
astray.

- Rumi

Forgiveness is the fragrance that the
violet sheds on the heel that has crushed
it.

- Mark Twain

The effect you have on others is the most
valuable currency there is.

- Jim Carrey

Until we have seen someone's darkness
we don't really know who they are.
Until we have forgiven someone's
darkness we don't really know what love
is.

- Marianne Williamson

Even after all this time the Sun never
says to the Earth, "You owe me." Look
what happens with a love like that, it
lights the whole sky.

- Hafiz

Our journeys are never straight, but they are always perfect.

- Jennifer Grant

No tree, it is said, can grow to heaven
unless its roots reach down to hell.

- Carl Jung

Life isn't about finding yourself. Life is
about creating yourself.

-George Bernard Shaw

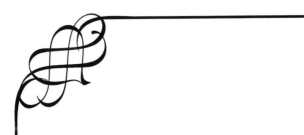

Most folks are as happy as they make up their minds to be.

- Abraham Lincoln

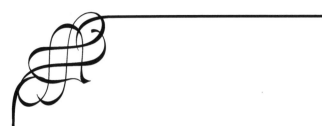

Our greatest glory is not in never falling,
but in rising every time we fall.

- Confucius

When you follow your bliss, the universe will open doors where there were only walls.

- Joseph Campbell

The act of forgiving yourself shows you
are living the awakened life.

- Wayne Dyer

The dark no longer has to have a deep hold and instead is just a guiding post of where we can add more light, more love.

- Jennifer Grant

In the end only three things matter: how
much you loved, how gently you lived,
and how gracefully you let go of things
not meant for you.

- Buddha

If you are not astonished that you exist,
your humanity is not complete.

- Deepak Chopra

You are very powerful, provided you
know how powerful you are.

- Yogi Bhajan

Strength does not come from winning,
your struggles develop your strengths.
When you go through hardships and
decide not to surrender, that is strength.

- Mahatma Gandhi

Leading with love starts from within,
otherwise there is no love at all.

- Jennifer Grant

❧ Acknowledgments ❧

Thank you to the many incredible people in my life that support me and my continued work. I am so grateful.

Special thanks for the inspiration of this book to Theresa Rose, my wonderful publishers Jaqueline Kyle and Caren Glasser, and the gal helping me feel beautiful in my clothing Jodi Mayers of Corset Styling.

To the HR Director that will bring this little book into her team meetings as a dose of inspiration – thank you. To the President of the organization that shares this work with her colleagues – thank you. To the single mom making life work and using this as inspiration – thank you. To the families that gather around and create new memories while discussing a quote – thank you.

To my two favorite people, my daughter Jasny and my fella Lindsey, thank you for continuously showing me what it truly means to lead with love. I am blessed.

❧ About the Author ❧

Jennifer is the founder of Inspiring Radiance where her mission is to spread the message of love and hope. After spending 32 years convinced she wasn't enough, she decided that was enough. Through her work as a speaker, writer and workshop leader, she is dedicated to supporting others and on a mission to lead with love. Realizing the need to take her message even further, Jennifer wrote her first book, *Dying to be Good Enough*, to share exactly what she did to change her life.

Additionally, Jennifer is the co-host of the "Happy, Healthy and Fit Life" podcast and has been a featured expert on KARE 11 News in Minneapolis.

Jennifer's diverse background includes working for a top non-profit, real estate, direct sales, and criminal justice. She entered college with the desire to help others by being an FBI Agent and even worked at an all-male maximum security prison. Jennifer is grateful her life experiences pointed her to a new path and her desire shifted to one filled with love.

An avid student of life, she is an Integrative Nutrition Health Coach and is also a KRI Certified Kundalini Yoga Instructor. She travels locally and nationally as a speaker, coach and workshop leader and loves every minute of it!

When she's not "working", you might find her reading, walking in nature, baking, practicing yoga, or strapping on her helmet for a motorcycle ride.

To learn more, please visit www.LoveJenGrant.com

 Book Jennifer Grant

to Speak at Your Next Meeting or Event:

"When it comes to speaking, Jennifer is simply amazing. She has a rare ability to capture and connect with an audience on a deep, personal level. You just 'get it' when she speaks." — Justin Yule, Co-Owner Chanhassen Fitness Revolution & Fitness Business Coach

"Her work is a great mix of inspiration, empowerment and fun!" - Anita Underberg, 2013-2014 President, MSOPA

Having Jen create and deliver a program for your organization will help each member of your team focus on what is needed for growth. By understanding their personal and professional challenges along with their many strengths, they will be empowered to engage with their work, take actions that lead to better results and stay accountable going forward. The best part, by knowing themselves better, they are happier!

Jen helps organizations foster happy and productive teams. She uses proven tools and systems to reduce stress and inspire action. She is an author, speaker, and workshop leader and also a Kundalini Yoga and Meditation Instructor and holds a certificate as a Holistic Health Coach. Using her philosophy to Lead with Love, her memorable and motivating messages are like a dose of honey for your soul and organization.

Jen says, "When we live from a place of peace, we are relaxed and embody the creative truth of who we are which leads to measurable personal and professional results."

For availability and booking information, feel free to contact Jen directly at Jen@LoveJenGrant.com or visit www.LoveJenGrant.com for more information.

Tater Tot Hotdish for the Heart

Prep/Cook Time: 30 minutes
Bake Time: 60-70 minutes

Ingredients:
1 medium onion, diced
3 medium carrots, diced
1-2 cloves garlic, minced
1 lb. ground beef
1/2 bunch of kale, stems removed and chopped
1-14.5 oz can green beans, drained and chopped
1-14 oz can mushroom soup (we use Amy's soup – mushroom bisque)
1/4 cup half and half (or other dairy/non-dairy option)
1 bag frozen tater tots (we use Alexia Gluten Free Potato Puffs)
Salt and Pepper
Other spices as you choose (we like paprika, chili powder, sage, and thyme)

Pre-heat oven to 350 degrees.

In a large skillet, warm 2 tablespoons oil over medium heat. Add onions, carrots and salt and pepper to taste. Let soften approximately 15 minutes while stirring occasionally. Add minced garlic, ground beef and other spices you prefer. Stir occasionally allowing to brown while scraping the bottom of your pan. Just before the ground beef is cooked through, add the chopped kale and stir.

Once softened and beef is cooked through, remove from heat and spread evenly in the bottom of your dish. I prefer my square 8X8 dish (in the cover photo). Layer the chopped green beans evenly over the ground beef mixture. In a small bowl, mix the soup with the half and half and pour evenly over the top of the green beans. With the back of a spoon, gently smooth the mixture in the pan. Top with a layer of tater tots. Bake at 350 for 60-70 minutes. When done, the mixture will be slightly bubbly and the tots will be lightly browned.

It will be extremely hot – be careful. Enjoy!!